Esther

Esther is such an exciting story.
It is from the Old Testament part of the Bible.
The story of Esther is full of drama and suspense,
and has many lessons that we can learn
from to help us in our lives today.

Getting started

Hi

You may have never really read the Bible before, but we are so glad that you are now.
God says that He wants to talk to us from His Word (the Bible) – so here goes!
Try to read a section each day – it will only take a few minutes. Find somewhere quiet,
where you won't be disturbed or distracted.

Each day,

1 *Pray a short prayer, asking God to help you understand the text you are going to read.*

2 *Read the Bible passage first. (You will find all the Bible passages at the end of this book). Then read the page from your notes.*

3 *Think about what you have read.*

4 *Have a go at answering the questions.*

5 *In a short prayer, ask God to help you put into practice what you have learnt from the story. If you have learnt something about God or Jesus, praise and thank Him. Spend a short time praying about people you know, and your day ahead.*

6 *Don't be tempted to rush ahead on to the next day!*

A royal party

Esther 1:1–8

This very rich and powerful Persian king seemed to have everything the world could offer. The party he held lasted for 187 days!

? *Can you describe the courtyard where the king held the party?*

....

? *How much wine were his visitors allowed to drink?*

....

....

The answer is NO

Queen Vashti was having her own party, but was rudely interrupted. The king, who was now very drunk, commanded her to come to his party so that he could show off her beauty to all the men there. She refused, which was the right thing to do.

Why was the king very happy? (v 10)

....

What makes you happy?

....

What makes you angry?

....

I'll get my own back!

It is easy when we are angry to try to get our own back. The king did just that. He was angry with Queen Vashti for not obeying him. The other mistake he made was to ask advice from the wrong people.

? *When you are upset, who do you ask for advice?*

....

? *What did Queen Vashti lose as a result of disobeying the king? (v 19)*

....

DAY 4

Beauty queen contest

Isn't it amazing how we can be persuaded to do something wrong if we like the idea?

 What did the king's servants suggest to him? (v2)

....

 How should the king have replied to their suggestion?

....

Jews in a foreign land

The people of Persia did not worship God, but there were Jewish people living in Susa who were God's people. They loved and worshipped God. Mordecai was a Jew, and he had adopted a young orphan girl, who was his cousin. She was called Esther.

? *What did Esther look like? (v 7)*

....

? *What tribe was Mordecai from ? (v 5)*

....

40 days with **Esther**

A Jewish contestant

Esther 2:8–9

Many girls entered the contest to be the next queen, and Esther was one of them.

Who was put in charge of looking after the girls? (v 8)

....

....

Esther pleased those looking after her. What special favours was she given? (v 9)

....

....

....

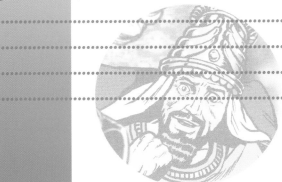

days with **Esther**

Secrets and salons

Esther was a Jew. She and her family worshipped God. Mordecai, her cousin, had told her not to tell anyone that she was a Jew, as the Persian people didn't like the Jews. She did as he asked. Mordecai cared about Esther and was concerned for her.

? *How often did Mordecai walk back and forth near the courtyard where Esther stayed? (v 11)*

....

? *How many months of beauty treatment did the girls have before appearing before the king? (v 12)*

....

40 days with Esther

Beauty and the beast

Being beautiful is more than what a person looks like. Esther was beautiful in looks, but also in character. Everyone liked her (v 15). The king was pleased with her and chose her to be his queen.

? *What did the king do in order to celebrate Esther being queen? (v 18)*

....

? *Why do you think the king chose Esther as queen?*

....

Plots and punishment

Esther 2:19–23

40 days with Esther

? What had Esther learnt to do since she was very young? (v 20)

It was right to obey Mordecai, as he was a wise man and obeyed God. Mordecai overheard two of the king's officers planning to kill the king. Mordecai told Esther to tell the king. The king's officers were punished and Esther told the king that it was Mordecai who had saved his life.

? What was written in the presence of the king? (v 23)

Promotion and pride

Haman was a wicked, selfish man, but the king gave him a high position, which meant all the people had to bow down to him.

Who was the only person who refused to bow down? (v 2)

....

The Jewish people worshipped only God and could not bow down to anyone or anything else.

Do you think that Mordecai would obey God or Haman?

....

40 days with Esther

Getting his own back

Haman had no respect for the Jewish people's beliefs or for God. He was so angry because Mordecai would not bow to him, that he looked for a way of killing all the Jewish people who lived in the kingdom.

? *Who did Haman go to so that he could kill the Jews? (v 8)*

....

? *What lies did Haman tell the king about the Jews? (v 8)*

....

? *How much silver did Haman offer to the king for the killing of the Jews? (v 9)*

....

40
days with
Esther

Signed and sealed

Do you think people learn from their mistakes? King Xerxes certainly didn't. Again, he was listening to the wrong people and acting without thinking.

? *How did the Jews throughout the kingdom know that Haman was going to kill them? (v 13)*

....

? *What did the king and wicked Haman do after the messengers had set out? (v 15)*

Torn clothes and tears

When Mordecai heard about what was going to happen to his people, the Jews, he went to the king's gate and cried loudly. He tore his clothes and put some rough ones on, to show how sad he was. All the Jewish people did the same and stopped eating. This was what they did when they wanted to pray and plead for God's help.

? Who was the only one who could help these people?

....

? Did God care about what was happening to his people?

....

Esther 4:4–7

When Esther heard that her cousin Mordecai was very upset, she was concerned for him. She sent him new clothes to wear.

Are you concerned when people you love are hurting? What do you do to help them?

....

Esther sent her servant to ask Mordecai why he was upset.

Why was Mordecai upset? (v 7)

....

Esther 4:8–11

Sceptres and secrets

DAY **15**

Mordecai sent a copy of the letter that said all the Jews were to be killed, to Esther. He asked her to go to the king and plead for his mercy towards her people, the Jews.

? *Why was Esther afraid to go to the king? (v 11)*

....

? *Who were Queen Esther's people?*

....

Esther 4:12–14

God is in control

Mordecai again sent a message to Esther for help. Many years before, God had promised Mordecai's ancestor, Abraham, that He would send a deliverer for His people the Jews. Mordecai believed God's promises and knew that God would not allow His people, the Jews, to be completely destroyed. He knew that if Esther didn't help, then God would provide someone else.

? *Why did Mordecai think that Esther had been chosen to be queen? (v 14b)*

....

? *Who has a perfect plan for all our lives?*

....

If I die, I die

Esther 4:15–17

Esther very bravely agreed to go to the King and beg for his mercy for her people, the Jews. She very wisely asked all the people to fast and pray before she went to the king.

? *Why was this a wise thing for Esther to ask?*

....

? *For how many days did Esther ask the Jews to fast and pray?*

....

40 *days with* **Esther**

Worry turns to wonder

Esther 5:1–4

How brave Esther was! She put on her best dress and went to see the king. Amazingly, he was pleased to see her, and she invited him to a party with wicked Haman.

What did the king hold out to Esther, to show her that he wanted to see her? (v 2)

....

Who was with Esther and was looking after her?

....

days with Esther

Esther 5:5–8

Party mood

Esther was patiently waiting for the right time to talk to the king about her people, the Jews. She invited the king and wicked Haman to another party the following day.

? *Are you patient like Esther, or do you rush into things when you want something?*

....

? *What did the king offer Esther? (v 6)*

....

40 days with Esther

Pride comes before a fall

Haman was very proud of his wealth, his possessions and his important job for the king. He bragged before his family about all he had achieved. But, one thing spoilt it for him – Mordecai refused to bow before him. This made him very angry.

When you do well, perhaps in a test at school, or have nice things, do you brag to others or do you thank God?

....

What did Haman's wife tell him to build? (v 14)

....

Who was Haman to build it for? (v 14)

....

40 days with Esther

A sleepless night

Esther 6:1–3

40 days with Esther

That same night, the king couldn't sleep. He read the daily court record and realised that Mordecai had never been rewarded for saving his life some time previously.

? *Who do you think caused the king to have a sleepless night?*

....

? *What was the job of the two men who had planned to kill the king? (v 2)*

....

Wrong place, wrong time

Have you ever been in the wrong place at the wrong time? In our reading today, Haman was! He'd come to tell tales about Mordecai and to try to get his own back on him, but it was going to backfire on him big time!

? *What had Haman come to ask the king? (v 4)*

....

? *Do you ever feel that you want to hurt people and get your own back? How do you think this makes God feel?*

....

40 days with Esther

Too big for his own boots

What a bighead Haman was! He had such a high opinion of himself that he thought the king was talking about him when the king asked how he could reward someone! What a shock he was going to get!

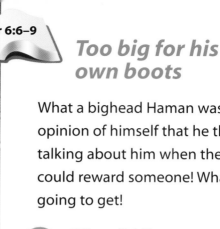 *What did Haman say the rewarded man should wear? (v 8)*

....

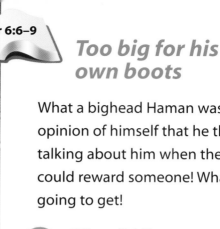 *What did Haman say the rewarded man should ride on through the city square? (v 9)*

....

40 days with Esther

Surprise, surprise

Shock, horror! The king told Haman to do all these good things to Haman's enemy, Mordecai!

? *How do you think Haman was feeling about all this?*

....

? *How do you think you might have felt if it was you?*

....

40 days with Esther

Poor old Haman. It must have been the worst day of his life – leading Mordecai through the streets and saying nice things about him.

Do you think Haman was sorry for hating Mordecai and the Jews?

....

Why do you think that Haman obeyed the king's command?

....

Esther 6:12–14

40 days with Esther

Haman went home very embarrassed, and told his family all that had happened. Haman's wife recognised that you can't fight God's people – the Jews – and win.

What was Haman's wife called? *(v 13)*

....

While Haman was talking to his family, the king's servants came to his home. Where did they take him? *(v 14)*

....

The final party

Queen Esther entertained the king and Haman, and explained to the king that she was a Jew, and that she was to be killed, along with all her people. She asked him to spare their lives.

? *Who was Esther trusting in when she made this request to the king?*

....

? *How do you think Esther was feeling?*

....

40
days with
Esther

The truth is out

The king wanted to know who had made these terrible plans to kill all the Jews. Esther told him it was Haman.

? *Why was Haman filled with fear? (v 6)*

....

? *Who do you think was in control?*

....

40 days with Esther

DAY 29

Trouble in store

Esther 7:7–8

The king was very angry. Haman was in big trouble and begged Esther to save his life. This got him into even bigger trouble.

? *Where did the king go to calm down from his anger? (v 7)*

....

....

....

? *What did the king see when he returned? (v 8)*

....

....

....

40 days with Esther

Esther 7:9–10

Poor old Haman ended up getting punished on the platform he built for Mordecai.
We need to be careful when we do evil things because evil may come back to us!

? How high was the platform that Haman died on? (v 9)

....

? Whose house was the platform near? (v 9)

....

40 days with Esther

You can't take it with you

Haman had gained a lot of money and material things in his life, but now he was dead, and he had left them all behind. The king gave everything that Haman had to Esther. She then put Mordecai in charge of all these things.

? *What did the king give to Mordecai?* (v 2)

....

? *What is most important in life: to have riches and many things, or to live to please God?*

....

40 *days with* Esther

Pleas and plans

Again, Esther pleaded with the king to do something so that her people, the Jews, wouldn't be killed. The king wanted to change Haman's wicked plans, but he couldn't, as even the king could not change the law.

? *Who had thought up the evil plans to kill the Jews? (v 3)*

....

? *Who is the only one who can change people's hearts and lives?*

....

40 days with Esther

Esther 8:7–8

The king agreed to write a new order to help all the Jewish people, so they wouldn't be wiped out. The king now wanted to do good to God's people, the Jews, and not evil.

? *What was used to seal the king's order? (v 8)*

....

? *What did the seal from the ring mean? (v 8)*

....

40 days with Esther

Letters galore

Lots of letters were written with the king's new orders. All the letters were sealed with the king's ring, so the order would not be changed.

? *How many different areas were the king's letters sent to? (v 9)*

....

? *How did Mordecai get the letters posted quickly? (v 10)*

....

days with *Esther*

Esther 8:11–14

Armed and ready

One problem remained because the king's order could never be cancelled. The king needed to add another order. This was that the Jews were to protect themselves and destroy any of their enemies.

? *Who did the Jews need to trust in to save them?*

....

? *How did the Jewish people know they would not be wiped out?*

....

From rags to royal robes

How things had changed! Mordecai was put in charge of all the king's orders. When the Jews saw him dressed in royal clothes with a crown on his head, they rejoiced. All the people feared the Jews, because they knew that God was with them.

? *What colour were Mordecai's clothes?* (v 15)

....

? *Why did many people become Jews?* (v 17)

....

When the day arrived for the Jews to be killed, they were all ready to protect themselves. Even some of their enemies helped them. God helped them to win the battle. Mordecai had become very important in the kingdom. He was fair and kind, not like Haman. He trusted in God.

? *In what month did the battle begin? (v 1)*

....

? *What did the Jews not take? (v 10)*

....

A king's pardon

Esther 9:11-17

The king bent over backwards to help Esther and the Jewish people. He granted all that she requested of him. All of Haman's wicked sons were killed because they were enemies of the Jews. People watched them die.

Who was hanged on Haman's platform? *(v 13–14)*

....

How many sons did Haman have? *(v 13–14)*

....

More letters!

To remember this wonderful victory and the safety of the Jews, Mordecai and Esther wrote lots of letters. These were to tell all the Jews to celebrate on the fourteenth and fifteenth day of the twelfth month every year. Their sadness was turned to joy. God had taken care of them.

? *Who do you think the Jewish people praised each year at this celebration?*

....

? *What was this celebration called? (v 26)*

....

40 days with Esther

Good men are remembered

The wicked king, Xerxes, became a great king, and all the good things he did were written down and remembered. Mordecai was remembered too for all the good he did for others.

? *All that we do in this life is seen by God and written in His book. Will you be proud or ashamed when that book is opened?*

? *Who was the most important Jew at this time? (v 3)*

Esther Bible text

Day 1 Chapter 1

1 This is what happened during the time of King Xerxes. He was the king who ruled the 127 areas from India to Cush.

2 In those days King Xerxes ruled from his capital city of Susa.

3 In the third year of his rule, he gave a banquet. It was for all his important men and royal officers. The army leaders from the countries of Persia and Media were there. And the important men from all Xerxes' empire were there.

4 The banquet lasted 180 days. All during that time King Xerxes was showing off the great wealth of his kingdom. And he was showing his own honour and greatness.

5 When the 180 days were over, the king gave another banquet. It was held in the courtyard of the palace garden for seven days. It was for everybody in the palace at Susa, from the greatest to the least important.

6 The courtyard had fine white curtains and purple drapes. These were tied to silver rings on marble pillars by white and purple cords. And there were gold and silver couches. These were on a floor set with tiles of white marble, shells and gems.

7 Wine was served in gold cups of various kinds. And there was plenty of the king's wine because he was very generous.

8 The king commanded that each guest be permitted to drink as much as he wished. He had told the wine servers to serve each man what he wanted.

Day 2

9 Queen Vashti also gave a banquet. It was for the women in the royal palace of King Xerxes.

10 On the seventh day of the banquet, King Xerxes was very happy because he had been drinking much wine. He gave a command to the seven eunuchs who served him. They were Mehuman, Biztha, Harbona, Bigtha, Abagtha, Zethar, and Carcas.

11 He commanded them to bring him Queen Vashti, wearing her royal crown. She was to come to show her beauty to the people and important men. She was very beautiful.

12 The eunuchs told Queen Vashti about the king's command. But she refused to come. Then the king became very angry. His anger was like a burning fire.

Day 3

13 It was a custom for the king to ask advice from experts about law and order. So King Xerxes spoke with the wise men. They would know the right thing to do.

14 The wise men the king usually talked to were Carshena, Shethar, Admatha, Tarshish, Meres, Marsena, and Memucan. They were seven of the important men of Persia and Media. These seven had special privileges to see the king. They had the highest rank in the kingdom.

15 The king asked those men, "What does the law say must be done to Queen Vashti? She has not obeyed the command of King Xerxes, which the eunuchs took to her."

16 Then Memucan spoke to the king and the other important men. He said, "Queen Vashti has not done wrong to the king alone. She has also done wrong to all the important men and all the people in all the empire of King Xerxes.

17 All the wives of the important men of Persia and Media will hear about the queen's actions. Then they will no longer honour their husbands. They will say, 'King Xerxes commanded Queen Vashti to be brought to him. But she refused to come.'

18 Today the wives of the important men of Persia and Media have heard about the queen's actions. And they will speak in the same way to their husbands. And there will be no end to disrespect and anger.

19 "So, our king, if it pleases you, give a royal order. And let it be written in the laws of Persia and Media, which cannot be changed. The law should say Vashti is never again to enter the presence of King Xerxes. Also let the king give her place as queen to someone who is better than she is.

20 And let the king's order be announced everywhere in his large kingdom. Then all the women will respect their husbands, from the greatest to the least important."

21 The king and his important men were happy with this advice. So King Xerxes did as Memucan suggested.

22 He sent letters to all the areas of the kingdom. A letter was sent to each area, written in its own form of writing. And a letter was sent to each group of people, written in their own language. These letters announced that each man was to be the ruler of his own family. Also, each family was to speak the language of the man.

Day 4 Chapter 2

1 Later, King Xerxes was not so angry. Then he remembered Vashti and what she had done. And he

Continued

remembered his order about her.

2 Then the king's personal servants had a suggestion. They said, "Let a search be made for beautiful young virgins for the king.

3 Let the king choose supervisors in every area of his kingdom. Let them bring every beautiful young virgin to the palace at Susa. These women should be taken to the women's quarters and put under the care of Hegai. He is the king's eunuch in charge of the women. And let beauty treatments be given to them.

4 Then let the girl who most pleases the king become queen in place of Vashti." The king liked this advice. So he did as they said.

Day 5

5 Now there was a Jewish man in the palace of Susa. His name was Mordecai son of Jair. Jair was the son of Shimei. And Shimei was the son of Kish. Mordecai was from the tribe of Benjamin.

6 Mordecai had been taken captive from Jerusalem by Nebuchadnezzar king of Babylon. Mordecai was part of the group taken into captivity with Jehoiachin king of Judah.

7 Mordecai had a cousin named Hadassah, who had no father or mother. So Mordecai took care of her. Hadassah was also called Esther, and she had a very pretty figure and face.

Mordecai had adopted her as his own daughter when her father and mother died.

Day 6

8 The king's command and order had been heard. And many girls had been brought to the palace in Susa. They had been put under the care of Hegai. When this happened, Esther was also taken to the king's palace. She was put into the care of Hegai, who was in charge of the women.

9 Esther pleased Hegai, and he liked her. So Hegai quickly began giving Esther her beauty treatments and special food. He gave her seven servant girls chosen from the king's palace. Then Hegai moved Esther and her seven servant girls to the best part of the women's quarters.

Day 7

10 Esther did not tell anyone about her family or who her people were. Mordecai had told her not to.

11 Every day Mordecai walked back and forth near the courtyard. This was where the king's women lived. He wanted to find out how Esther was and what was happening to her.

12 Before a girl could take her turn with King Xerxes, she had to complete twelve months of beauty treatments. These were ordered for the women. For six months she was treated with oil and myrrh. And she spent six months with perfumes and cosmetics. 13 Then she was ready to go to the king. Anything she asked for was given to her. She could take it with her from the women's quarters to the king's palace. 14 In the evening she would go to the king's palace. And in the morning she would return to another part of the women's quarters. There she would be placed under the care of a man named Shaashgaz. Shaashgaz was the king's eunuch in charge of the slave women. The girl would not go back to the king again unless he was pleased with her. Then he would call her by name to come back to him.

Day 8

15 Esther daughter of Abihail, Mordecai's uncle, had been adopted by Mordecai. The time came for Esther to go to the king. She asked for only what Hegai suggested she should take. (Hegai was the king's eunuch who was in charge of the women.) And everyone who saw Esther liked her. 16 So Esther was taken to King Xerxes in the royal palace. This happened in the tenth month, the month of Tebeth. It was in Xerxes' seventh year as king.

17 And the king was pleased with Esther more than with any of the other girls. And he liked her more than any of the other virgins. So King Xerxes put a royal crown on Esther's head. And he made her queen in place of Vashti. 18 Then the king gave a great banquet for Esther. He invited all his important men and royal officers. He announced a holiday in all the empire. And he was generous and gave everyone a gift.

Day 9

19 Now Mordecai was sitting at the king's gate. This was when the virgins were gathered the second time. 20 And Esther had still not told anyone about her family or who her people were. That is what Mordecai had told her to do. She still obeyed Mordecai just as she had done when he was bringing her up. 21 Now Bigthana and Teresh were two of the king's officers who guarded the doorway. While Mordecai was sitting at the king's gate, Bigthana and Teresh became angry at the king. And they began to make plans to kill King Xerxes.

Continued

22 But Mordecai found out about their plans and told Queen Esther. Then Queen Esther told the king. She also told him that Mordecai had found out about the evil plan.

23 When the report was investigated, it was found to be true. The two officers who had planned to kill the king were hanged. And all this was written down in the daily court record in the king's presence.

Day 10 *Chapter 3*

1 After these things happened, King Xerxes honoured Haman son of Hammedatha the Agagite. He gave Haman a new rank that was higher than all the important men.

2 And all the royal officers at the king's gate would bow down and kneel before Haman. This was what the king had ordered. But Mordecai would not bow down, and he did not kneel.

3 Then the royal officers at the king's gate asked Mordecai, "Why don't you obey the king's command?"

4 And they said this to him every day. When he did not listen to them, they told Haman about it. They wanted to see if Haman would accept Mordecai's behaviour because Mordecai had told them that he was Jew.

Day 11

5 Then Haman saw that Mordecai would not bow down to him or kneel before him. And he became very angry.

6 He had been told who the people of Mordecai were. And he thought of himself too important to try to kill only Mordecai. So he looked for a way to destroy all of Mordecai's people, the Jews, in all of Xerxes' kingdom.

7 It was in the first month of the twelfth year of King Xerxes' rule. That is the month of Nisan. Pur (that is, the lot) was thrown before Haman. The lot was used to choose a day and a month. So the twelfth month, the month of Adar, was chosen.

8 Then Haman said to King Xerxes, "There is a certain group of people in all the areas of your kingdom. They are scattered among the other people. They keep themselves separate. Their customs are different from those of all the other people. And they do not obey the king's laws. It is not right for you to allow them to continue living in your kingdom.

9 If it pleases the king, let an order be given to destroy those people. Then I will pay 345 tons of silver to those who do the king's business. They will put it into the royal treasury."

Day 12

10 So the king took his signet ring off and gave it to Haman. Haman son of Hammedatha, the Agagite, was the enemy of the Jews.

11 Then the king said to Haman, "The money and the people are yours. Do with them as you please."

12 On the thirteenth day of the first month, the royal secretaries were called. They wrote out all of Haman's orders. They wrote to the king's governors and to the captains of the soldiers in each area. And they wrote to the important men of each group of people. The orders were written to each area in its own form of writing. And they were written to each group of people in their own language. They were written in the name of King Xerxes and sealed with his signet ring.

13 Letters were sent by messengers to all the king's empire. They stated the king's order to destroy, kill, and completely wipe out all the Jews. That meant young and old, women and little children, too. The order said to kill all the Jews on a single day. That was to be the thirteenth day of the twelfth month, which was Adar. And it said to take all the things that belonged to the Jews.

14 A copy of the order was to be given out as a law in every area. It was to be made known to all the people so that they would be ready for that day.

15 The messengers set out, hurried by the king's command. At the same time the order was given in the palace at Susa. And the king and Haman sat down to drink. But the city of Susa was in confusion.

Day 13 Chapter 4

1 Now Mordecai heard about all that had been done. To show how upset he was, he tore his clothes. Then he put on rough cloth and ashes. And he went out into the city crying loudly and very sadly.

2 But Mordecai went only as far as the king's gate. This was because no one was allowed to enter that gate dressed in rough cloth.

3 The king's order reached every area. And there was great sadness and loud crying among the Jews. They gave up eating and cried out loudly. Many Jews lay down on rough cloth and ashes to show how sad they were.

Day 14

4 Esther's servant girls and eunuchs came to her and told her about Mordecai. Esther was very upset and afraid. She sent clothes for Mordecai to put on instead of the rough cloth. But he would not wear them.

Continued

5 Then Esther called for Hathach. He was one of the king's eunuchs chosen by the king to serve her. Esther ordered him to find out what was bothering Mordecai and why.

6 So Hathach went to Mordecai. Mordecai was in the city square in front of the king's gate.

7 Then Mordecai told Hathach everything that had happened to him. And he told Hathach about the amount of money Haman had promised to pay into the king's treasury for the killing of the Jews.

Day 15

8 Mordecai also gave him a copy of the order to kill the Jews, which had been given in Susa. He wanted Hathach to show it to Esther and to tell her about it. And Mordecai told him to order Esther to go into the king's presence. He wanted her to beg for mercy and to plead with him for her people.

9 Hathach went back and reported to Esther everything Mordecai had said.

10 Then Esther told Hathach to say to Mordecai,

11 "All the royal officers and people of the royal areas know this: no man or woman may go to the king in the inner courtyard without being called. There is only one law about this. Anyone who enters must be put to death. But if the king holds out his gold sceptre, that person may live. And I have not been called to go to the king for 30 days."

Day 16

12 And Esther's message was given to Mordecai.

13 Then Mordecai gave orders to say to Esther: "Just because you live in the king's palace, don't think that out of all the Jews you alone will escape.

14 You might keep quiet at this time. Then someone else will help and save the Jews. But you and your father's family will all die. And who knows, you may have been chosen queen for just such a time as this."

Day 17

15 Then Esther sent this answer to Mordecai:

16 "Go and get all the Jews in Susa together. For my sake, give up eating. Do not eat or drink for three days, night and day. I and my servant girls will also give up eating. Then I will go to the king, even though it is against the law. And if I die, I die."

17 So Mordecai went away. He did everything Esther had told him to do.

Day 18 Chapter 5

1 On the third day Esther put on her royal robes. Then she stood in the inner courtyard of the king's palace, facing the king's hall. The king was sitting on his royal throne in the hall, facing the doorway.
2 The king saw Queen Esther standing in the courtyard. When he saw her, he was very pleased. He held out to her the gold sceptre that was in his hand. So Esther went up to him and touched the end of the sceptre.
3 Then the king asked, "What is it, Queen Esther? What do you want to ask me? I will give you as much as half of my kingdom."
4 Esther answered, "My king, if it pleases you, come today with Haman to a banquet. I have prepared it for him."

Day 19

5 Then the king said, "Bring Haman quickly so we may do what Esther asks."
So the king and Haman went to the banquet Esther had prepared for them.
6 As they were drinking wine, the king said to Esther, "Now, Esther, what are you asking for? I will give it to you. What is it you want? I will give you as much as half of my kingdom."

7 Esther answered, "This is what I want and ask for.
8 My king, I hope you are pleased with me. If it pleases you, give me what I ask for and do what I want. Come with Haman tomorrow to the banquet I will prepare for you. Then I will answer your question about what I want."

Day 20

9 Haman left the king's palace that day happy and content. Then he saw Mordecai at the king's gate. And he saw that Mordecai did not stand up or tremble with fear before him. So Haman became very angry with Mordecai.
10 But he controlled his anger and went home. Then Haman called his friends and Zeresh, his wife, together.
11 And he told them about how wealthy he was and how many sons he had. He also told them all the ways the king had honoured him. And he told them how the king had placed him higher than his important men and his royal officers.
12 "And that's not all", Haman added. "I'm the only person Queen Esther invited to come with the king to the banquet she gave. And tomorrow also the queen has asked me to be her guest with the king.
13 But all this does not really make me happy. I'm

Continued

not happy as long as I see that Jew Mordecai sitting at the king's gate."

14 Then Haman's wife Zeresh and all his friends said, "Have a platform built to hang someone. Build it 25 metres high. And in the morning ask the king to have Mordecai hanged on it. Then go to the banquet with the king and be happy." Haman liked this suggestion. So he ordered the platform to be built.

Day 21 Chapter 6

1 That same night the king could not sleep. So he gave an order for the daily court record to be brought in and read to him.

2 And it was found recorded that Mordecai had warned the king about Bigthana and Teresh. These men had planned to kill the king. They were two of the king's officers who guarded the doorway.

3 Then the king asked, "What honour and reward have been given to Mordecai for this?" The king's personal servants answered, "Nothing has been done for Mordecai."

Day 22

4 The king said, "Who is in the courtyard?" Now Haman had just entered the outer court of the king's palace. He had come to ask the king about hanging Mordecai on the platform he had prepared.

5 The king's personal servants said, "Haman is standing in the courtyard."
So the king said, "Bring him in."

Day 23

6 So Haman came in. And the king asked him, "What should be done for a man that the king wants very much to honour?" And Haman thought to himself, "Whom would the king want to honour more than me?"

7 So he answered the king, "This is what you could do for the man you want very much to honour.

8 Have the servants bring a royal robe that the king himself has worn. And also bring a horse with a royal crown on its head. The horse should be one that the king himself has ridden.

9 Then let the robe and the horse be given to one of the king's most important men. Let the servants put the robe on the man the king wants very much to honour. And let them lead him on the horse through the city streets. As they are leading him, let them announce: 'This is what is done for the man the king wants very much to honour!'"

Day 24

10 The king commanded Haman, "Go quickly. Take the robe and the horse just as you have said. And do all this for Mordecai the Jew who sits at the king's gate. Do not leave out anything you have suggested."

Day 25

11 So Haman took the robe and the horse. And he put the robe on Mordecai. Then he led him on horseback through the city streets. Haman announced before Mordecai: "This is what is done for the man the king wants very much to honour!"

Day 26

12 Then Mordecai went back to the king's gate. But Haman hurried home with his head covered. He was embarrassed and ashamed.
13 He told his wife Zeresh and all his friends everything that had happened to him.
Haman's wife and the men who gave him advice said, "You are starting to lose power to Mordecai. Since he is a Jew, you cannot win against him. You will surely be ruined."

14 While they were still talking, the king's eunuchs came to Haman's house. They made Haman hurry to the banquet Esther had prepared.

Day 27 *Chapter 7*

1 So the king and Haman went in to eat with Queen Esther.
2 They were drinking wine. And the king said to Esther on this second day also, "What are you asking for? I will give it to you. What is it you want? I will give you as much as half of my kingdom."
3 Then Queen Esther answered, "My king, I hope you are pleased with me. If it pleases you, let me live. This is what I ask. And let my people live, too. This is what I want.
4 I ask this because my people and I have been sold to be destroyed. We are to be killed and completely wiped out. If we had been sold as male and female slaves, I would have kept quiet. That would not be enough of a problem to bother the king."

Day 28

5 Then King Xerxes asked Queen Esther, "Who is he? Where is he? Who has done such a thing?"

Continued

6 Esther said, "A man who is against us! Our enemy is this wicked Haman!"
Then Haman was filled with terror before the king and queen.

Day 29
7 The king was very angry. He got up, left his wine and went out into the palace garden. But Haman stayed inside to beg Queen Esther to save his life. He could see that the king had already decided to kill him.
8 The king came back from the palace garden to the banquet hall. And he saw Haman falling on the couch where Esther was lying. The king said, "Will he even attack the queen while I am in the house?" As soon as the king said that, servants came in and covered Haman's face.

Day 30
9 Harbona was one of the eunuchs there serving the king. He said, "Look, a platform for hanging people stands near Haman's house. It is 25 metres high. This is the one Haman had prepared for Mordecai, who gave the warning that saved the king."
The king said, "Hang Haman on it!"

10 So they hanged Haman on the platform he had prepared for Mordecai. Then the king was not so angry any more.

Day 31 *Chapter 8*
1 That same day King Xerxes gave Queen Esther everything Haman had left when he died. Haman had been the enemy of the Jews. And Mordecai came in to see the king. He came because Esther had told the king how he was related to her.
2 Then the king took off his signet ring, which he had taken back from Haman. And he gave it to Mordecai. Then Esther put Mordecai in charge of everything Haman had left when he died.

Day 32
3 Once again Esther spoke to the king. She fell at the king's feet and cried. She begged the king to stop the evil plan of Haman the Agagite. Haman had thought up the plan against the Jews.
4 The king held out the gold sceptre to Esther. Esther got up and stood in front of the king.
5 She said, "My king, I hope you are pleased with me. And maybe it will please you to do this. You might

think it is the right thing to do. And maybe you are happy with me. If so, let an order be written to cancel the letters Haman wrote.

6 I could not stand to see that terrible thing happen to my people. I could not stand to see my family killed."

Day 33

7 King Xerxes answered Queen Esther and Mordecai the Jew. He said, "Because Haman was against the Jews, I have given his things to Esther. And my soldiers have hanged him.

8 Now write another order in the king's name. Write it to the Jews as it seems best to you. Then seal the order with the king's signet ring. No letter written in the king's name and sealed with his signet ring can be cancelled."

Day 34

9 At that time the king's secretaries were called. This was done on the twenty-third day of the third month, which is Sivan. The secretaries wrote out all of Mordecai's orders. They wrote to the Jews and to the governors and to the captains of the soldiers in each area. And they wrote to the important men of the 127 areas which reached from India to Cush.

They wrote to each area in its own form of writing. And they wrote to each group of people in their own language. They also wrote to the Jews in their own form of writing and their own language.

10 Mordecai wrote orders in the name of King Xerxes. And he sealed the letters with the king's signet ring. Then he sent the king's orders by messengers on horses. The messengers rode fast horses, which were raised just for the king.

Day 35

11 These were the king's orders: the Jews in every city have the right to gather together to protect themselves. They have the right to destroy, kill and completely wipe out the army of any area or people who attack them. And they are to do the same to the women and children of that army. The Jews also have the right to take by force the property of the enemies.

12 The one day set for the Jews to do this was the thirteenth day of the twelfth month. This was the month of Adar. They were allowed to do this in all the empire of King Xerxes.

13 A copy of the king's order was to be sent out as a law in every area. It was to be made known to the

Continued

people of every nation living in the kingdom. This was so the Jews would be ready on that set day. The Jews would be allowed to pay back their enemies. 14 The messengers hurried out, riding on the royal horses. The king commanded those messengers to hurry. And the order was also given in the palace at Susa.

Day 36

15 Mordecai left the king's presence wearing royal clothes. They were blue and white. And he had on a large gold crown. He also had a purple robe made of the best linen. And the people of Susa shouted for joy.

16 It was a time of happiness, joy, gladness and honour for the Jews.

17 The king's order went to every area and city. And there was joy and gladness among the Jews. This happened in every area and city to which the king's order went. The Jews were having feasts and celebrating. And many people through all the empire became Jews. They did that because they were afraid of the Jews.

Day 37 *Chapter 9*

1 The order the king had commanded was to be done on the thirteenth day of the twelfth month. That was the month of Adar. That was the day the enemies of the Jews had hoped to defeat them. But that was changed. So the Jews themselves defeated those who hated them.

2 The Jews met in their cities in all the empire of King Xerxes. They met in order to attack those who wanted to harm them. And no one was strong enough to fight against them. This was because all the other people living in the empire were afraid of Jews.

3 And all the important men of the areas, the governors, captains of the soldiers, and the king's officers helped the Jews. They helped because they were afraid of Mordecai.

4 Mordecai was very important in the king's palace. He was famous in all the empire. This was because he was becoming a leader of more and more people.

5 And, with their swords, the Jews defeated all their enemies, killing and destroying them. And the Jews did what they wanted with those people who hated them.

6 In the palace at Susa, they killed and destroyed 500 men.

7 They also killed these men: Parshandatha, Dalphon,

Aspatha,
8 Poratha, Adalia, Aridatha,
9 Parmashta, Arisai, Aridai, and Vaizatha,
10 They were the ten sons of Haman, son of Hammedatha, the enemy of the Jews. But the Jews did not take their belongings.

Day 38

11 And on that day the number of the men killed in the palace at Susa was reported to the king.
12 The king said to Queen Esther, "The Jews have killed and destroyed 500 men in the palace at Susa. And they have also killed Haman's ten sons. What have they done in the rest of the king's empire! Now what else are you asking? I will do it! And what else do you want? It will be done."
13 Esther answered, "If it pleases the king, give the Jews in Susa permission to do this. Let them do again tomorrow what the king ordered for today. And let the bodies of Haman's ten sons be hanged on the platform built for hanging people to death."
14 So the king ordered that it be done. A law was given in Susa, and the bodies of the ten sons of Haman were hanged.
15 The Jews in Susa came together. It was on the fourteenth day of the month of Adar. And they killed 300 men in Susa. But they did not take their belongings.

16 At that same time, the other Jews in the king's empire also met. This was to protect themselves and get rid of their enemies. And they killed 75,000 of those who hated them. But they did not take their belongings.
17 This happened on the thirteenth day of the month of Adar. And on the fourteenth day the Jews rested. They made it a day of joyful feasting.

Day 39

18 But the Jews in Susa met on the thirteenth and fourteenth days of the month of Adar. Then they rested on the fifteenth day. They made it a day of joyful feasting.
19 This is why the Jews who live in the country and small villages celebrate on the fourteenth day. They keep the fourteenth day of the month of Adar as a day of joyful feasting. And it is also a day for giving presents to each other.
20 Mordecai wrote down everything that had happened. Then he sent letters to all the Jews in all the empire of King Xerxes. He sent letters to places far and near.
21 Mordecai did this to have the Jews celebrate every year. They were to celebrate on the fourteenth

Continued

and fifteenth days of the month of Adar.

22 It was to celebrate a time when the Jews got rid of their enemies. They were also to celebrate it as the month their sadness was turned to joy. It was the month when their crying for the dead was turned into celebration. Mordecai wrote letters to all the Jews. He told them to celebrate those days as days of joyful feasting. It was to be a time of giving food to each other. And it was a time of giving presents to the poor.

23 So the Jews agreed to do what Mordecai had written to them. And they agreed to hold the celebration every year.

24 Haman son of Hammedatha, the Agagite, was the enemy of all the Jews. He had made an evil plan against the Jews to destroy them. And Haman had thrown the pur (that is, the lot) to choose a day to ruin and destroy the Jews.

25 But when the king learned of the evil plan, he sent out written orders. This was so the evil plans Haman had made against the Jews would be used against him. And those orders said that Haman and his sons should be hanged on the platform for hanging.

26 So these days were called Purim. The name Purim comes from the word "pur" (the lot).

27 And so the Jews set up this custom. They and their descendants would celebrate these two days every year. The Jews and all those who join them are to celebrate these two days. They should do it without fail every year. They should do it in the right way and at the time Mordecai had ordered them in the letter.

28 These two days should be remembered and celebrated from now on in every family. And they must be celebrated in every area and every city. These days of Purim should never stop being celebrated by the Jews. And the descendants of the Jews should always remember to celebrate these two days of Purim.

29 So Queen Esther daughter of Abihail, along with Mordecai the Jew, wrote this second letter about Purim. Using the power they had, they wrote to prove the first letter was true.

30 And Mordecai sent letters to all the Jews in the 127 areas of the kingdom of Xerxes. Mordecai wrote a message of peace and truth.

31 He wrote to set up these days of Purim. They are to be celebrated at their chosen times. Mordecai the Jew and Queen Esther had sent out the order for the Jews. They had set up for themselves and their descendants these two days. They set them up so the Jews would give up eating and cry loudly.

32 Esther's letter showed that these practices about Purim were correct. They were written down in the records.

Day 40 *Chapter 10*

1 King Xerxes made people pay taxes. Even the cities far away on the seacoast had to pay taxes.
2 And all the great things that Xerxes did are written down. They tell of his power and strength. They are written in the record books of the kings of Media and Persia. Also written in those record books are all the things that Mordecai did. The king had made Mordecai a great man.
3 Mordecai the Jew was second in importance to King Xerxes. He was the most important man among the Jews. And his fellow Jews respected him very much. They respected Mordecai because he worked for the good of his people. And they respected him because he spoke up for the safety of all the Jews.

First Published 2005 by
Visual Impact Resources Ltd
7 Silverton Drive
Stenson Fields
Derby
DE24 3BU
ISBN 1-86024-550-1

Design by
Ben Kennedy

Produced in the EU by
Print by Design Ltd
16 Castle Street, Bodmin
Cornwall
PL31 2DU
Tel: 0845 226 7306

If you have enjoyed following the *40 days with Esther* daily reading scheme, then why not try another from our 'daily readings' series.

70 days with Mark has all the same features as *40 days with Esther*, including a suggested daily reading from the Bible with helpful comments and questions by Sue Hudson.

70 days with Mark will take you through the whole Gospel of Mark in ten weeks, and includes 70 full colour Bible illustrations. *70 days with Mark* (ISBN 1-86024-536-6) Available from all Christian bookshops or from the Visual Impact Resources website:

www.visual-impact-resources.co.uk

For details of our **Amazing 3D Bible Storybooks,** you can visit our website, or just turn over the page!

International Children's Bible
New Century Version

The International Children's Bible is different. It is not an adult Bible with a children's cover, nor is it an abridged version of adult text or a 'storybook' Bible. The ICB stands alone as the only totally new translation of the original Bible text – from the Greek and Hebrew language – specifically for children.

Hardback: 0-8500-9901-3   **Paperback:** 0-8500-9900-5

International Children's Bible – New Testament
New Century Version

This New Testament edition of the International Children's Bible includes delightful full-colour artwork and almost 100 black and white illustrations within the Bible text which makes the ICB text even easier to follow and understand for the 6–10-year-old reader. Also included: dictionary of Bible terms, colour maps, ICB family tree and translation notes.

Hardback: 1-86024-431-9   **Paperback:** 1-86024-432-7

Amazing 3D Bible Story Books

These picture books bring Bible stories to life. Just pop on the attached glasses and see the amazing depth of the 3D illustrations, which will surely engage the minds of children and help them remember Bible stories.
Each book contains one free 3D Viewer!

Stories include *Jonah and the Big Fish, David and Goliath, Miracles of Jesus, and Parables of Jesus.*
Miracles of Jesus: 1-86024-504-8 **Parables of Jesus:** 1-86024-505-6 **David & Goliath:** 1-86024-507-2
Jonah & the Big Fish: 1-86024-506-4
Available from all Christian bookshops or visit our website at: **www.visual-impact-resources.co.uk**